# The Truth (& Myths) about American Heroes

## by L. A. Peacock

## illustrated by Jon Davis

Scholastic Inc.

To the students, faculty, and staff of the New Bedford Adult Learning Center, who inspire me every day—L.A.F.

Text copyright © 2016 by L.A. Peacock
Illustrations copyright © 2016 by Scholastic Inc.

The publisher does not have any control over and does not assume any responsibility for author or third-party websites or their content.

ISBN 978-0-545-83027-0

10 9 8 7 6 5 4 3            16 17 18 19 20

Printed in the U.S.A.            40

First printing 2016
Book design by David Neuhaus

# Contents

# Pocahontas
## 1595? – 1617

## Was Pocahontas really a princess?

Yes, she was a daughter of Powhatan. Her father was the powerful chief of thirty Indian tribes in eastern Virginia during the early 1600s.

## What happened in 1607?

About one hundred colonists arrived from England to settle in Powhatan's territory. They built Jamestown, the first **permanent** English colony, near present-day Richmond. One of the leaders was Captain John Smith.

## How did Pocahontas become a hero?

Pocahontas visited the colony often and brought food. She helped the colonists **survive** the long winter of 1607, when she was about twelve.

# Did Pocahontas know Captain John Smith?

Yes, she was his teacher. Smith learned to translate English sentences into the Indian language. Smith also taught Pocahontas the colonists' language and customs.

## TRUTH or MYTH?

### Pocahontas saved John Smith's life.

**MYTH!** Probably not. In 1609, Smith was taken captive by Powhatan's warriors. Smith wrote years later in his book that Pocahontas had begged her father to let him live. We don't know if this famous story is true. But Smith was let go.

# Were the settlers and Indians always friendly?

No. In 1612, the two sides fought, and Pocahontas was held as a **hostage**. She became a Christian and took the name Rebecca. She also met and married John Rolfe, an English settler who wanted to import tobacco to Europe.

ROLFE CREATED A MIX OF INDIAN TOBACCOS TO SELL TO EUROPE.

THIS NEW CROP MADE HIM RICH.

# What did Powhatan give the happy couple for a wedding present?

A lot of land, a string of pearls, and eight years of peace for the colony. In 1616, the couple traveled to England with their two-year-old son.

# Whom did Pocahontas meet in England?

King James I. Pocahontas was a big hit. She spoke English. The king and queen liked her clothes and manners. Pocahontas proved that the New World was a good place to send more English colonists. Pocahontas had her **portrait** painted wearing her fancy new clothes.

# What did King James like to collect?

Strange plants and animals from the New World. One of his favorite things from the colonies was a pair of flying squirrels from the Virginia forest.

WATCH OUT!

# Did Pocahontas return to Jamestown?

No. She planned to return, but she got sick with smallpox. She died around the age of twenty-two and was buried in England.

☆ ☆ ☆ ☆ ☆ ☆ ☆ ☆ ☆ ☆

# Benjamin Franklin
## 1706 – 1790

# What famous documents did Franklin sign?

He was the only Founding Father to sign the Declaration of Independence, the U.S. Constitution, and the Treaty of Paris, which ended the American Revolutionary War.

# Was Benjamin Franklin a bestselling author?

Yes, he wrote and published *Poor Richard's Almanack*, one of the most popular books in the American colonies.

# Why did Franklin retire at the age of 42?

*Poor Richard* made Franklin a rich man. He wanted to spend more time doing science experiments and helping his country.

# Was he a genius?

A lot of people thought so. Franklin was not only a famous writer and businessman but also a scientist, an inventor, a musician, a **diplomat**, and a patriot.

**Franklin is credited with creating the first . . .**

a) *glass armonica (a musical instrument made of glass pieces).*

b) *lightning rod.*

c) *Franklin refrigerator.*

d) *bifocal glasses.*

e) *electrical battery.*

The answers are *a, b, d,* and *e.* He didn't invent the fridge, but he did create the Franklin stove, the efficient woodburning stove still in use today.

# Why did Franklin fly a kite in a thunderstorm?

He wanted to prove that lightning was a form of electricity. It was his most famous experiment.

# Did Franklin go to England in 1764?

He spent about ten years there, fighting for the rights of the thirteen colonies. In April 1775, while Franklin was sailing home, the Revolutionary War started. Franklin became one of its leaders.

# Why did the seventy-year-old Franklin go to France in 1776?

To get help from France in America's fight against the powerful British army and navy.

# Did the French help the Americans win the Revolutionary War?

Yes. France sent ships, money, and supplies to the Americans. Franklin—the famous scientist and inventor—was a big hit in Europe. The king admired the fur hat that Franklin wore to the French court!

☆ ☆ ☆ ☆ ☆ ☆ ☆ ☆ ☆ ☆

# George Washington
## 1732 – 1799

## Who was called the "Father of His Country?"

George Washington, the first president of the United States. He was the commanding general of the American forces in the Revolutionary War and led the new nation to victory over the British.

## Was Washington always a soldier?

No. He was born the son of a rich Virginia farmer. Washington was good at math. He **surveyed** the family farm at the age of fourteen. Later, he helped map the wilderness of the Shenandoah Valley.

# When did Washington's military life begin?

When he was twenty-one, Washington joined the Virginia militia and fought in the French and Indian War. At twenty-six, he quit the army and returned to his Virginia plantation, Mount Vernon. He was called back to duty to lead the American army in the Revolutionary War.

WASHINGTON SHOWED COURAGE AND CALM IN BATTLE.

HE WAS KNOWN AS A GREAT LEADER.

## TRUTH or MYTH?

**Washington organized a spy network to defeat the British.**

**TRUTH!** He used clever spies and surprise attacks to defeat the enemy.

# Why did Washington's army stop fighting in December 1777?

It was winter. Washington took his army of 11,000 to Valley Forge, north of Philadelphia. Roughly 2,000 American soldiers died in camp from hunger, cold, and disease. But under Washington's leadership, the army kept training. By spring, the men were ready to battle the British and win the war.

# Why did Washington leave his Virginia home again in 1787?

To lead the Constitutional Convention in Philadelphia and help plan the new U.S. government. The former general and war hero was everyone's choice for president of the new country. Washington took the oath of office on April 30, 1789.

# Did Washington always keep his mouth closed for official portraits?

Yes. He had only one of his original teeth. Washington had lost most of his teeth to gum disease. He wore false teeth made mostly from human teeth and hippopotamus ivory.

# Did George Washington ever live in Washington, D.C.?

No, but he helped select the site on the Potomac River where the new federal Capitol was built.

THE CITY WAS NAMED IN HIS HONOR.

WASHINGTON LIVED IN THE EARLY CAPITALS OF NEW YORK AND PHILADELPHIA.

# What's the tallest structure in Washington, D.C.?

The Washington Monument, at 555 feet. By law, no building in the nation's capital can be taller.

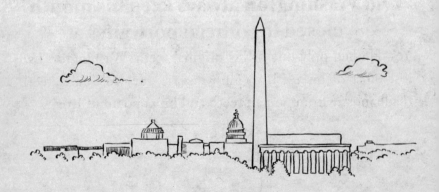

## Meriwether Lewis
### 1774 – 1809

## William Clark
### 1770 – 1838

# How did the United States double in size in 1803?

With the Louisiana Purchase. France sold the Louisiana Territory to President Thomas Jefferson. This huge piece of land stretched from the Mississippi River to the Rocky Mountains. It was unmapped and dangerous wilderness, filled with unknown plants, animals, and Indian tribes.

LOUISIANA PURCHASE, 1803

# What special job did Jefferson give to Captain Meriwether Lewis?

Jefferson asked Lewis to lead a group of explorers, a "Corps of Discovery," to explore the vast new territory to the Pacific Ocean. Meriwether chose William Clark, a skilled mapmaker, to be his co-captain. York, Clark's African American slave, and Seaman, a huge black Newfoundland dog, came with them.

## What did Jefferson ask them to do?

To make maps and keep records of all the new plants and animals they found. Like Jefferson, Lewis was curious about the new frontier. The territory was largely unknown to white people.

## Did Lewis and Clark meet any other people on their journey?

Indian tribes lived in the new territory. Most were friendly. The explorers gave the Indians presents from President Jefferson.

CAN WE HAVE THE DOG, TOO?

# Who helped guide the explorers?

Sacagawea, a teenage Shoshone Indian girl. With her newborn son on her back, Sacagawea guided the expedition through the unknown territory. She communicated with the other tribes, identified native plants, and traded for the horses they needed to cross the Rocky Mountains.

# How long did it take Lewis and Clark to cross the Rockies?

Eleven days. They almost froze to death. It took them one year, six months, and one day to reach the Pacific Ocean in November 1805. They were the first U.S. citizens to cross the American continent.

**At the end of their 8,000-mile journey to the Pacific and back, Lewis and Clark had discovered:**

a) 122 animals

b) 178 plants

c) around 50 Indian tribes

d) 18 lakes

The answers are *a*, *b*, and *c*. They wanted to cross the continent river by river, but they didn't find the Northwest Passage. It didn't exist.

# What gifts did they send back to President Jefferson?

Thousands of new plants and animals, including live birds and a prairie dog.

## Harriet Tubman
### 1820? – 1913

# Who was the best-known **conductor** on the Underground Railroad?

The ex-slave Harriet Tubman. Born on a Maryland plantation, she risked her life to escape in 1849 along the Underground Railroad. She followed the North Star by night, hid by day, and walked a hundred miles to Philadelphia and freedom.

# Was the Underground Railroad a subway train?

No, it wasn't below ground. It was a secret network of hiding places known as "safe houses." The Railroad ran along the route from slave states in the South to free northern states and Canada.

# Who helped the runaway slaves?

Abolitionists. These people were against slavery. They ran the safe houses, hid the escaped slaves, and carried them secretly in their wagons.

# Did Tubman stay long in Philadelphia?

Only long enough to save money and travel back to Maryland. She rescued her sister and her sister's children, and guided them north. It was the first of many trips in which she led escaped slaves along the Underground Railroad.

# Why did Tubman carry a rifle on her rescue trips?

To stop a runaway slave from changing his or her mind. Tubman pointed her gun and warned, "Go on, or die." Once a slave got on the Underground Railroad, there was no turning back.

# Why was there a $40,000 reward for Harriet Tubman's capture?

Slaveholders wanted to stop Tubman. She had made nineteen trips on the Underground Railroad, helping 300 slaves escape to Canada.

HARRIET TUBMAN WAS KNOWN AS MOSES.

JUST LIKE THE BIBLICAL LEADER WHO LED HIS PEOPLE OUT OF SLAVERY.

Harriet Tubman was a Civil War spy.

**TRUTH!** She worked for Union colonel James Montgomery. Tubman organized a scouting party along the waterways of South Carolina before his troops arrived on the scene.

# What did Tubman do after the Civil War?

She married a black veteran named Nelson David and settled on a small farm in New York. Tubman raised money for schools for former slaves. Later, her farm became a home for older African Americans. She died of pneumonia in 1913, around the age of 93.

## Did Tubman fight against other injustices?

Yes. She fought for women's voting rights in her later years.

HARRIET TUBMAN WAS A LONGTIME FRIEND OF SUFFRAGIST SUSAN B. ANTHONY.

# Abraham Lincoln
## 1809 – 1865

# Why is Lincoln often called the greatest American president?

Because of his many **achievements**. Lincoln held the nation together through a bloody Civil War, **abolished** slavery in America, and strengthened the federal government and the economy.

## TRUTH or MYTH?

Lincoln was the first president to be born in a log cabin.

**MYTH!** Andrew Jackson was, in 1767. Like Jackson, Lincoln was born in a log cabin on the frontier and grew up poor. Lincoln's mother died when he was nine. Neither of his parents could read or write.

WAAAAAA

## What did Lincoln do before he entered politics at age 25?

He had a lot of different jobs. Lincoln worked as a store clerk, a postmaster, a flatboat **navigator**, a rail-splitter, and a soldier in the army.

## What happened just after Lincoln became president in 1860?

Six slaveholding states in the South **seceded**, or left, the Union. They formed a new government called the Confederate States of America. Jefferson Davis was elected their first president. Within six months, five other states left the Union and joined the Confederacy.

## Was Lincoln able to keep the Union together?

No, but he tried. Confederate troops attacked Union forces at Fort Sumter in Charleston, South Carolina. The Civil War began.

# How bad was the Civil War?

It was the bloodiest war in American history. About 620,000 people on both sides died from disease and battle wounds.

**What new technologies were first used in the Civil War?**

a) Telegraph for communication

b) Battleships covered with iron

c) Railroads to transport troops

d) Hot air balloons for spying

e) Mines and hand grenades

*All of the above.* Trenches and foxholes to fight battles were also used widely during the Civil War.

## Did Lincoln's Emancipation Proclamation free the slaves?

Not all of them. A law was needed, not just Lincoln's official statement, to abolish slavery in rebel states. After the Civil War, the Thirteenth Amendment to the Constitution was passed, outlawing slavery everywhere.

## At what event did Lincoln give his famous Gettysburg Address?

At the dedication of a cemetery on the Civil War battlefield at Gettysburg, Pennsylvania.

☆ ☆  ☆ ☆ ☆ ☆ ☆ ☆ ☆ ☆

# Frederick Douglass
## 1818 – 1895

# What changed the life of eight-year-old Frederick Douglass?

He learned to read.

## Why was that so unusual?

Frederick was a slave. In the early 1800s, it was against the law to teach a slave to read and write. Mrs. Auld, his Baltimore owner, didn't know the law. Her husband made her stop teaching Frederick.

## Did Frederick stop reading?

No, it was too late. Young Frederick continued to read old newspapers in secret. He learned about the growing antislavery **movement**.

# How did Frederick escape from slavery?

He ran away to New York City when he was twenty. Frederick married Anna Murray, a free black woman, and moved to New Bedford, Massachusetts.

HE TOOK THE NAME OF DOUGLASS AND WORKED IN LOCAL SHIPYARDS.

HE JOINED THE ABOLITIONIST MOVEMENT...

...AND ATTENDED ANTISLAVERY MEETINGS.

## How did he become famous?

Douglass gave powerful speeches about his life as a slave. Over the years, he gave hundreds of speeches. Douglass called for the end of slavery and often left his audiences in tears.

## TRUTH or MYTH?

**Douglass was a conductor on the Underground Railroad.**
**TRUTH!** He directed a branch of the Railroad. He helped slaves to escape, including the runaway Henry "Box" Brown, who had arrived in Philadelphia from Virginia in a crate.

# Was Douglass in danger of being captured as a runaway slave?

Always, especially after he wrote his autobiography, *Narrative of the Life of Frederick Douglass*, in 1845. The book made him more famous, selling 30,000 copies in the United States and England.

# Did Douglass fight in the Civil War?

No, but his two sons did. Douglass helped recruit black soldiers for the Union Army.

## Did he meet President Lincoln?

Yes. Douglass asked the president to bring an end to slavery.

# What did Douglass do after the Civil War?

He continued to fight for reforms and equal rights, including voting rights for black Americans. Douglass died in 1895.

☆ ☆  ☆ ☆ ☆ ☆ ☆ ☆ ☆ ☆

# Susan B. Anthony
## 1820 – 1906

## How did Susan B. Anthony get her start as a reformer?

She got fired from her teaching job in New York State. Susan protested when she found out that she was paid one-quarter of what male teachers earned.

## What else did she fight for?

She was against the drinking of liquor. **Temperance** supporters believed that men drunk on alcohol caused the problems of poverty and abuse of women and children.

## When did she join the fight for women's rights?

In 1851, when she met Elizabeth Cady Stanton. The two women became a great team in the **suffrage** movement, fighting for a woman's right to vote.

# What legal rights did American women have in the 1800s?

Not many. A woman was little more than her husband's property.

**According to early 1800s law, a married woman's husband:**

a) owned all her property.

b) kept all the money she earned.

c) had control of the children.

d) could abuse her anytime.

*All of the above.* Also, a woman couldn't serve on a jury, sign a contract, go to college, or vote in elections.

# Why was the right to vote important?

If women couldn't vote, they couldn't help change the laws that held them back.

# What was Anthony and Stanton's first big achievement?

In 1860, the suffragettes got the New York State legislature to give married women the right to own property, to have joint custody of their children, and to be able to keep the money they earned.

## TRUTH or MYTH?

**The Fifteenth Amendment to the Constitution guaranteed all citizens the right to vote.**

**MYTH!** Only male citizens could vote. Under the new law, former slaves could now vote. This right was based on race and color, not gender.

# What did Anthony do to break the law on November 5, 1872?

She voted in the presidential election. Immediately, she was put in jail and tried.

THE JUDGE FOUND HER GUILTY.

SHE NEVER PAID THE $100 FINE.

ARRESTED MISS SUSAN B. ANTHONY FOR VOTING

# How long before women got the right to vote?

That took a lot longer to achieve. After the slaves won their freedom, suffragettes pushed for an **amendment** to the Constitution to give women the vote.

# Did Anthony live to see voting rights for women?

No, she died in 1902. In 1920, the Nineteenth Amendment was passed, giving all women in America the right to vote.

☆ ☆ ☆ ☆ ☆ ☆ ☆ ☆ ☆ ☆

# Sitting Bull
## 1831?–1890

# What Indian chief was called Tatanka Iyotanka?

"Sitting Bull," the translation of his Lakota Sioux name. This famous Great Plains warrior was also called "Slow" because of his serious manner.

## What did Sitting Bull do around the age of ten?

He killed his first buffalo. Four years later, he fought his first battle against an enemy tribe.

## TRUTH or MYTH?

Sitting Bull held two jobs with his tribe.

**TRUTH!** He was both a fierce war chief and a holy medicine man. For the Sioux, holy men were honored. The Indians believed that they communicated with the spirit world.

# Why was Sitting Bull a hero to his people?

He led the Lakota against the U.S. government in the fight to save Indian lands and their way of life.

HE FOUGHT TO KEEP WHITE MEN OUT OF THE BLACK HILLS OF SOUTH DAKOTA.

THESE LANDS WERE SACRED TO THE SIOUX.

# Why did outsiders want to take over the Black Hills?

Gold was discovered there in 1874. The U.S. broke its treaty with the Indians. The government sent the army to drive the Indians off their own land. Sitting Bull and his followers refused to leave.

# Whom did Sitting Bull fight alongside?

Crazy Horse, another famous Plains Indian chief. These two war chiefs led their people and defended their homeland against the U.S. cavalry.

# What was the Sioux's biggest victory in the Plains Indian War?

The Battle of Little Bighorn in 1876. Sitting Bull and Crazy Horse led 2,500 Sioux warriors into battle against U.S. lieutenant colonel George Armstrong Custer and his 215 armed men.

## How long did the battle last?

About one hour. It was later called Custer's Last Stand. All his men died near Sitting Bull's camp near the Little Bighorn River.

## Why was the Indian victory short-lived?

Custer's defeat angered the American people. The government sent more troops until the chiefs surrendered.

# What happened to Sitting Bull?

He took his people across the border to Canada in 1877. They hunted buffalo for a while. Sitting Bull surrendered when his people began to starve. The chief went to jail for two years. His people were held as prisoners on a **reservation** in South Dakota.

## How did "Buffalo Bill" Cody make Sitting Bull famous?

The showman got the chief to join his Wild West Show in 1885. For four months, Sitting Bull toured all over the United States as a celebrity.

## When did Sitting Bull die?

In 1890, while he was being arrested again. A gunfight broke out, and Sitting Bull was shot.

# Alexander Graham Bell
## 1847 – 1922

# What did Alexander Graham Bell consider to be his life's work?

It wasn't the telephone. Bell said it was teaching speech to the deaf.

# How did he learn about the science of speech?

It ran in the Bell family. Both his father and grandfather were speech teachers.

# Who was the first inventor in the family?

Bell's father, Melville. He studied how the voice produces sounds.

MELVILLE INVENTED A UNIVERSAL PHONETIC ALPHABET.

THERE'S A **UNIQUE** SYMBOL FOR EACH HUMAN SOUND.

# Who taught Alexander his music?

Bell's mother played the piano, though she was almost deaf. His mother used an ear tube to hear, or feel, the music as it **vibrated** from the piano's soundboard. Young Alexander was curious. He was fascinated by the vibrating sounds made by the piano.

# What did Alexander discover when he played with musical tuning forks?

That each vowel had a different rate of vibration. Later, he learned that these unique sounds could pass through a wire. He was on his way to inventing the telephone.

## TRUTH or MYTH?

In 1875, Alexander Graham Bell built his first telephone.

**MYTH!** Bell made a drawing of the phone, but it was his twenty-one-year-old assistant, Thomas Watson, who turned Bell's idea into an actual machine.

# How did the first telephone work?

Voice sounds were changed into electric currents and then passed over a wire. A device at the end of the wire changed the electrical energy back into sounds.

# What were the first words spoken and heard over the telephone?

"Mr. Watson—Come here—I want to see you," spoke Alexander Graham Bell to his assistant in the next room in his Boston home on March 10, 1876.

THE NEW BELL TELEPHONE COMPANY WAS BORN.

# What happened next?

Bell and Watson began talking between Boston and Cambridge, two miles apart. Soon, people in Boston and New York City were having conversations. By the 1900s, telephones regularly linked New York and Chicago.

# When could you call from coast to coast?

Not until January 1915. It took a network of 130,000 telephone poles, across thirteen states, to make the call from New York to California.

## Wilbur Wright
### 1867 – 1912

## Orville Wright
### 1871 – 1948

# How did the Wright brothers make history?

They were the first to fly an airplane. The 1903 Wright Flyer was the first powered airplane to fly successfully.

## TRUTH or MYTH?

**The Wright brothers were trained in science and engineering.**

**MYTH!** They never finished high school. They were bicycle mechanics from Dayton, Ohio. As children, the brothers were fascinated by mechanical things. They loved taking their toys apart and putting them back together.

# When was the first airplane flight?

It took place on December 17, 1903, on the beach at Kitty Hawk, North Carolina. Their flyer had two wings and a small engine. The pilot lay on the lower wing to control the machine—up, down, and around.

# How did the brothers decide who would be the first to try to fly?

They flipped a coin. Wilbur won, but he was up for only three and a half seconds—not long enough to matter. When Orville took a turn, he reached 120 feet and flew for twelve seconds, the first real flight. They took more flights. Three days later, the longest flight lasted 59 seconds, with Wilbur as the pilot. The brothers proved that humans could actually fly.

## Were Wilbur and Orville ready to sell airplanes?

No, they left Kitty Hawk and went back to their bicycle shop in Dayton, Ohio, to build better planes.

## Did they succeed?

By 1905, their planes could fly for thirty-nine minutes. Soon, planes could fly up to twenty-five miles, take off and land **repeatedly**, and make circles in the sky.

THEY WANTED TO MAKE AND SELL PLANES.

IN 1908, THE US MILITARY BEGAN BUYING FLYERS.

## Did people believe the Wright brothers had actually flown at Kitty Hawk?

Not everyone, especially people in Europe. French pilots had flown their flying machines in front of big crowds of people. So Wilbur packed up the latest Flyer and headed for Le Mans, France. Between August 1908 and January 1909, he made more than 100 flights, took up 60 passengers, and became famous.

# What were their passengers like?

One passenger, Leon Bollée, was 240 pounds. Another was Madame Hart O. Berg, the first woman to fly. She tied a rope around her skirt so it wouldn't fly up.

# Where can you see the original 1903 Wright Flyer today?

It's on permanent display at the National Air and Space Museum, Smithsonian Institution, in Washington, D.C.

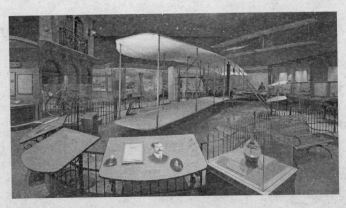

☆ ☆ ☆ ☆ ☆ ☆ ☆ ☆ ☆ ☆

# Helen Keller
## 1881 – 1968

## How did Helen Keller lose her sight and hearing?

An illness, probably scarlet fever, left her blind and deaf when she was almost two.

## How did Helen live?

She was trapped in a world without light and sound. Young Helen was angry and frightened. She couldn't communicate with people. She kicked, screamed, and had **temper tantrums**.

## What leader in deaf education examined six-year-old Helen?

Alexander Graham Bell. He told her parents to find a teacher for Helen at the Perkins Institution for the Blind in Boston. The school sent Annie Sullivan to the Keller family.

## How did Annie Sullivan help Helen?

She taught Helen a hand alphabet. Now Helen was able to communicate by spelling out words into a person's hands.

## What was the first word that Helen learned?

*Water*. Annie held Helen's hand under a water pump. In her other hand, Annie spelled out the word *water*. The world opened up to Helen. She learned many new words at amazing speed.

## What did Helen call Annie?

She finger-spelled the word T-E-A-C-H-E-R. They stayed together for the next 50 years.

HELEN RODE HORSES, SWAM, ROWED A BOAT, AND TOOK WALKS IN THE WOODS.

SHE EVEN LEARNED TO SPEAK A LITTLE.

## TRUTH or MYTH?

Helen learned to read books.

**TRUTH!** She read Braille—writing in which raised dots represent letters and numbers.

# Whom did Helen go to college with?

Annie Sullivan took classes with Helen at Radcliffe College. Annie signed the professor's **lectures** into Helen's hand.

# How do we know so much about Helen?

Helen wrote her autobiography, *The Story of My Life*, while in college. It was a bestseller. With Annie, she went on lecture tours throughout the world and became famous.

ANNIE DIED IN 1936.

A MOVIE CALLED 'THE MIRACLE WORKER' SHOWED HELEN'S LIFE WITH ANNIE.

## What happened to Helen?

She continued to meet people and travel the world. Helen raised money to help blind people. She visited soldiers in World War II. Helen gave hope to those who were blinded or made deaf in battle. She showed them that, like her, they could live a happy life. Helen was 87 years old when she died in 1968.

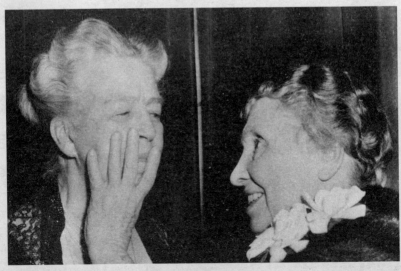

 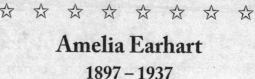

# Amelia Earhart
## 1897 – 1937

## How did Amelia cause a sensation in 1928?

She did something dangerous. She was the first woman to cross the Atlantic Ocean by plane.

## Did she fly the plane herself?

No, she was a passenger. But people thought it was a brave thing for a woman to do. Amelia became a national hero.

## Was this her first time in an airplane?

No. Her first ride was in 1920. She was excited. Amelia knew then that she had to pilot her own plane.

WHOOPEE!!!

# How did Amelia buy her first plane?

She borrowed the money from her mother. Amelia took flying lessons, got her pilot's license, and started flying in exhibitions and air circuses.

AMELIA WASN'T THE ONLY BRAVE WOMAN IN THE FAMILY.

HER MOTHER WAS THE FIRST WOMAN TO CLIMB PIKE'S PEAK IN COLORADO.

## TRUTH or MYTH?

Amelia Earhart was the first person to fly **solo** across the Atlantic Ocean.

**MYTH!** Charles Lindbergh made that historic flight from New York to Paris in 1927.

YOUR AMERICAN HEROES I.Q.

As an aviator, Amelia set many world records for women pilots, including being the first to:

*a) make a round-trip solo flight across the U.S.*

*b) fly over the Pacific, from Hawaii to California.*

*c) set a speed record flying nonstop from Mexico City to New York City.*

*d) fly solo on a transatlantic flight.*

*e) pilot a plane around the globe.*

The answers are *a*, *b*, *c*, and *d*. Amelia achieved many firsts for women, but she didn't fly around the world.

# When did she make the transatlantic flight alone?

In 1932, she flew solo from Newfoundland to Ireland. Her time was 13 hours, 30 minutes—a new record.

# Did she set a new record by flying around the world?

No, but she tried. On May 21, 1937, Amelia took off from California with her copilot, Fred Noonan. It was the start of a nearly 30,000-mile trip around the globe. But her plane disappeared mysteriously in the Pacific Ocean.

## What happened to the plane?

We're not sure. Amelia had taken off from New Guinea on July 2, 1937. The plane headed toward tiny Howland Island in the middle of the Pacific Ocean. An hour later, Amelia sent a radio message giving her position.

## Was the plane ever found?

No. Radio contact was lost. The plane went down in the South Pacific. For weeks, the military searched the area. There was no trace of the plane or crew. To this day, it's a mystery.

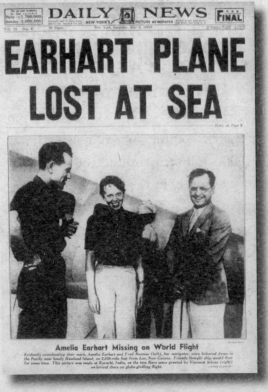

# Albert Einstein
## 1879 – 1955

## What equation unlocked the secret of the atom?

$E=mc^2$! Its author was the physicist Albert Einstein. His discovery that matter was **interchangeable** with energy brought on the nuclear age.

EINSTEIN IS FAMOUS FOR HIS THEORY OF RELATIVITY.

IT RELATES SPACE, TIME, AND GRAVITY.

THE THEORY TRIES TO SHOW HOW THE UNIVERSE WORKS.

## Was Einstein honored for his achievements?

Yes. He won the Nobel Prize for Physics in 1921. He was a genius, the most famous scientist of the time. In that year, he made his first visit to the United States and received a hero's welcome in New York City. Thousands greeted his ship. Crowds cheered as his motorcade drove to City Hall.

## What was driving scientists out of Germany in the 1930s?

Hitler and his Nazi soldiers. Because of Hitler's terrible actions against the Jews, many German scientists feared for their lives. Some escaped with their families to work in England and America.

## What did Einstein do?

He left Germany in 1932, never to return. He took a position at the Institute for Advanced Study at Princeton University in the United States.

## TRUTH or MYTH?

**Einstein drove to his Princeton University office each morning.**

**MYTH!** Einstein didn't drive. He walked to his office, often lost in thought. It became a town attraction to watch him **shuffle** down the street.

# Why was Einstein a big supporter of world peace?

He knew how terrible the Nazis were, particularly against the Jewish people. Previously, Einstein had spoken out against World War I. In his view, war was no way to settle conflicts. Now Einstein was worried about Hitler and events in Europe.

# Why did Einstein write President Franklin D. Roosevelt a letter in 1939?

World War II was coming. Einstein knew that Hitler was developing a **nuclear bomb**. He was afraid that Hitler would create and use this horrible weapon.

# What did Einstein urge Roosevelt to do?

Einstein convinced the president to act first and build America's own bomb.

## How did Einstein feel when the U.S. dropped atomic bombs on Japan to end World War II?

Terrible. He regretted sending that letter to Roosevelt. Einstein spent the rest of his life speaking out against nuclear war and fighting for **human rights**.

# Franklin Delano Roosevelt
## 1882 – 1945

## Which U.S. president served more than two terms?

Franklin Delano Roosevelt was elected four times. A few months into his fourth term, he died of a brain **hemorrhage**. Later, the Twenty-second Amendment was passed in 1951 limiting presidents to two terms.

## Did Roosevelt have a favorite chair?

Yes, a wheelchair. At the age of 39, he caught the disease polio and was **paralyzed** from the waist down. Sometimes Roosevelt wore braces to stand up to give speeches. However, he spent most of his time in a wheelchair.

# Who was Roosevelt's constant companion?

His black Scottie dog, Fala. The little dog was almost as famous as the president's wife, Eleanor.

# What did Roosevelt promise the American people?

A "New Deal." The 1930s was a difficult time. One out of four people was out of work. Many Americans were homeless and stood in long lines for food. In his first 100 days in office, FDR got Congress to pass new laws to lift the country out of the Great Depression.

**The New Deal proposed laws to:**

a) put people back to work.

b) help farmers.

c) provide free health care for the poor.

d) build new roads and dams.

e) give Social Security income to elderly citizens.

The answers are *a*, *b*, *d*, and *e*. Medicaid, the federal program to give free health care for poor children and families, was passed by President Lyndon B. Johnson in 1965.

# TRUTH or MYTH?

FDR grew up rich but fought to help poor people.

**TRUTH!** Roosevelt came from a wealthy family, but he dedicated his life to helping poor Americans.

FDR'S SPEECHES INSPIRED PEOPLE.

HE SAID, "THE ONLY THING WE HAVE TO FEAR IS FEAR ITSELF."

## How did Roosevelt explain his programs to the American people?

By his talks on the radio called "fireside chats." FDR's words gave people hope. They began to trust that the government would help them.

## What did FDR do after the Japanese bombed Pearl Harbor on December 7, 1941?

He led the nation into World War II. Roosevelt sent American troops to fight Hitler's army in Europe and Japanese forces in the Pacific.

## What important meeting happened in 1945?

FDR met with British prime minister Winston Churchill and Soviet leader Joseph Stalin to discuss an end to the war and to plan the future of a new Europe.

# Eleanor Roosevelt
## 1884 – 1962

## What president's wife changed the role of First Lady?

Eleanor Roosevelt. As FDR's wife, she used her position as First Lady to fight against poverty and racial injustice. Eleanor was a strong supporter for equal rights for women. As a **social activist,** she was probably the most influential woman of twentieth-century America.

## TRUTH or MYTH?

### Eleanor was always courageous and outspoken.

**MYTH!** As a child, she was shy, lonely, and afraid of the dark. At fifteen, she went to school in England. She gained confidence and learned to stand up for her beliefs.

## Who was her famous uncle?

Teddy Roosevelt, the Rough Rider and twenty-sixth U.S. president. It was Uncle Teddy who walked Eleanor down the aisle and gave her away on her wedding to Franklin, a distant cousin, in 1905.

## Was Eleanor busy during her first ten years of marriage?

Yes, she spent most of her time raising five children.

## In 1921, how did the world suddenly change for the Roosevelts?

Franklin became crippled by polio and lost the use of his legs. But Eleanor kept his political career alive. She gave speeches and traveled the country in his place. Eleanor became his "eyes and ears." She told him what she saw and heard.

## When Franklin was elected New York governor, what was Eleanor doing?

Eleanor organized women voters for the Democratic Party and helped get her husband elected U.S. president in 1932.

# What did she do two days after FDR took office as president?

Eleanor held her own press conference—a first for First Ladies. And only women journalists were allowed to attend. It was a way to get more newspapers to hire women reporters.

# Did Eleanor travel often as First Lady?

In FDR's first year in office, she traveled more than 40,000 miles.

# What did she talk about in her speeches?

Eleanor spoke about social reforms to end child labor and to increase the minimum wage. She visited coal mines, farmers, and poor people. Eleanor brought comfort and hope to millions of Americans across the country.

# How did Eleanor earn the title "First Lady of the World"?

She never stopped fighting against social injustice, even after her husband's death in 1945. She traveled the world on behalf of human rights.

## What important job did she have?

President Harry S. Truman appointed Eleanor the U.S. delegate to the new United Nations. In 1948, she helped the United Nations pass the Universal Declaration of Human Rights.

CHAIRMAN

## What was her last official position?

In 1961, Eleanor chaired President John F. Kennedy's Commission on the Status of Women. Eleanor died in New York City at the age of 78.

☆ ☆ ☆ ☆ ☆ ☆ ☆ ☆ ☆ ☆

# Rachel Carson
## 1907 – 1964

## How did Rachel Carson give the world a wake-up call in 1962?

She wrote a book called *Silent Spring*. She showed how chemical **pesticides**, which were being used to kill harmful insects, were poisoning the environment.

## What "song" would be silenced by chemicals?

The planet's many species of birds. Since the use of DDT, a dangerous pesticide, whole populations of birds were disappearing. In time, Carson warned, there would be "no songs in the air." People needed to learn about the dangers of harmful chemicals to their food and the environment.

## Why was *Silent Spring* an important book?

It changed people's view of the world. Nature needed to be protected. Many people believe that *Silent Spring* started the "save the environment" movement.

## Where did Rachel get her love of nature?

From her mother, a schoolteacher in Springdale, Pennsylvania. Later, Rachel became a marine biologist and worked for the U.S. Fish and Wildlife Service. In 1949, she became editor-in-chief of their publishing program.

## Was *Silent Spring* Rachel's first book?

No. She wrote *The Sea Around Us* in 1951. A bestseller, the book was translated into 28 languages and won the National Book Award.

# TRUTH or MYTH?

Everyone welcomed the success of *Silent Spring*.

**MYTH!** Not the big chemical companies. They made fun of Rachel. They called her a "**hysterical** woman." But millions read her powerful words about the dangers of pesticides.

# What event in 1957 led Rachel to write *Silent Spring*?

A letter from a friend asking for help. She told Rachel that the songbirds in her yard had died after a government plane sprayed her town for mosquitoes.

# What happened next?

Rachel became interested in **ecology** and chemical pollution. For the next four years, she collected data from scientists on the dangers of toxic chemicals on plants and animals around the globe. The result was the publication of *Silent Spring*.

# Which president read *Silent Spring*?

President Kennedy. Because of Rachel's work, a panel was formed to study the effects of pesticides on the environment. As a result, the government made new **regulations** to control the use of pesticides.

# Is DDT still used in the United States?

No, the use of the pesticide was banned by the Environmental Protection Agency in 1972.

☆ ☆ ☆ ☆ ☆ ☆ ☆ ☆ ☆ ☆

# Rosa Parks
## 1913 – 2005

## TRUTH or MYTH?

Rosa Parks stood up for civil rights by sitting down.
**TRUTH!** On December 1, 1955, Rosa refused to give up her seat on a bus so a white man could take her seat.

ROSA WASN'T JUST TIRED FROM HER JOB.

SHE WAS TIRED OF GIVING IN TO RACIAL INJUSTICE.

# Was Rosa arrested?

Yes, because she broke the law. Rosa was an African American woman living in a racially **segregated** southern state.

# What were "Jim Crow" laws?

In the 1950s, these were the laws in some states that separated black and white people in public areas such as bathrooms, restaurants, and city buses. When the buses were crowded, black people had to give up their seats to whites and stand in the back.

# How did black people pay their bus fares in Montgomery, Alabama?

They usually paid their fares to the driver at the front of the bus. Then they got off and used the back door to get back on the bus.

# Was Rosa the only black person to refuse to give up a seat?

Yes, the bus driver asked four black people to move. Only Rosa refused. The police were called and took her to jail.

# What did Rosa's arrest lead to?

A major **boycott** of city buses in Montgomery. Blacks walked, formed carpools, and took taxies. But they didn't take the buses. The bus company lost money, because 75 percent of bus riders were black people.

# How long was the bus boycott?

Over a year—381 days.

# Was the protest a success?

Yes. In 1956, the U.S. District Court declared that separate seats for blacks and whites on city buses were unconstitutional. This decision was upheld by the U.S. Supreme Court. Racial segregation in public transportation was finally at an end.

## Why was Rosa's brave act so important?

It was the spark that **ignited** the Civil Rights Movement. The Montgomery boycott showed that nonviolence and peaceful protest could successfully challenge racial injustice.

## How is Rosa Parks remembered?

She is known today as the "Mother of the Civil Rights Movement." Rosa continued her work against racial injustice for the rest of her life. She died at the age of 92 in 2005.

☆ ☆ ☆ ☆ ☆ ☆ ☆ ☆ ☆ ☆

# Jackie Robinson
## 1919 – 1972

# Who broke the color barrier in baseball?

Jackie Robinson. In 1946, he signed a contract with the all-white Montreal Royals, a farm team of the Brooklyn Dodgers (now the Los Angeles Dodgers).

# When was Jackie's first major league game?

A year later. On April 15, 1947, Jackie took first base for the Dodgers.

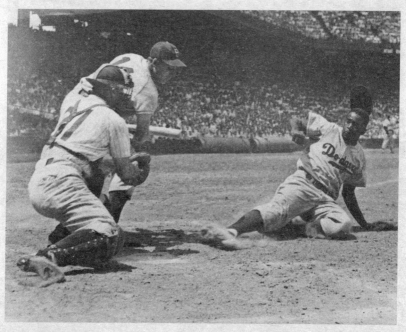

# TRUTH or MYTH?

**Before Jackie Robinson, African Americans had played professional baseball for years.**

**TRUTH!** But not in the big leagues. In the 1940s, baseball was divided by race. Many talented African Americans could only play in the segregated Negro leagues. The sixteen major league teams were for "whites only."

**YOUR AMERICAN HEROES I.Q.**

**In his lifetime, Jackie held a lot of different jobs, including:**

*a) lieutenant in the U.S. Army.*

*b) lawyer.*

*c) businessman.*

*d) baseball player.*

The answers are *a, c,* and *d.* He wasn't a lawyer, but he did speak out for equal opportunity for all people.

JACKIE WAS AN ALL-AMERICAN FOOTBALL PLAYER IN COLLEGE.

AND A STAR ATHLETE IN BASEBALL, BASKETBALL, AND TRACK.

# How did Branch Rickey change baseball forever?

He was president and general manager of the Brooklyn Dodgers. It was Rickey who asked Jackie to join the Dodgers and be the first black player to make major league history.

## Why did Rickey choose Jackie?

He thought that Jackie had the talent to succeed in the big leagues. Rickey also believed Jackie was strong enough to stand up to insults and death threats from racist fans.

## What advice did he give Jackie?

To control his anger. Rickey told Jackie that he was looking for a ballplayer "with guts enough *not* to fight back"!

## How well did Jackie play in the major leagues?

In his first Dodgers' season, Jackie had 175 hits and a .297 batting average. His 29 stolen bases led the league. Jackie was so good that he was named Rookie of the Year.

## Did the Dodgers win with Jackie?

He played for them for ten years. Jackie helped lead the team to six league championships. In 1949, the Dodgers won the World Series. Jackie batted .342 and was the National League MVP.

## When did Jackie retire?

After the 1956 season. Six years later, he became the first black player in the National Baseball Hall of Fame.

# Dr. Martin Luther King Jr.
## 1929 – 1968

## Who had "a dream" that changed the world?

The Reverend Dr. Martin Luther King Jr., when he gave his famous "I Have a Dream" speech on the steps of the Lincoln Memorial on August 28, 1963, in Washington, D.C. It was a turning point in America's fight for racial equality.

## TRUTH or MYTH?

About 250,000 Americans from across the country heard his speech.

**TRUTH!** King's powerful words reached the hearts of millions more through television and newspapers.

# Why was young Martin kicked out of first grade?

He told his teacher he was five. But he was too young for school, so he had to wait another year.

# What was Martin's profession?

He was trained as a minister. Martin graduated the top student in his **seminary** class. He got a doctorate degree in philosophy from Boston University, where he met Coretta Scott. They married in 1953. Dr. King joined his father as pastor at Atlanta's Ebenezer Baptist Church.

**YOUR AMERICAN HEROES I.Q.**

**When Martin was growing up, laws and customs in the South separated the races. Black and white people . . .**

a) went to separate schools.

b) served on all-white or all-black juries.

c) sat in different parts of the bus.

d) used their own restrooms.

e) were treated at separate hospitals.

f) ate in different restaurants.

*All of the above.* In some places, black people had to move off the sidewalk when a white person passed by.

# Who led the Montgomery bus boycott with Rosa Parks in 1955?

A twenty-six-year-old minister named Martin Luther King Jr. He used tactics of nonviolent protest. Dr. King taught blacks to hold their anger. They didn't fight back when racist people yelled, threatened, and often hit them.

DR. KING USED PEACEFUL METHODS TO FIGHT INJUSTICE.

HE LED THE CIVIL RIGHTS MOVEMENT.

# How did children marching in Birmingham, Alabama, in 1963 help the Civil Rights Movement?

Teenage girls and boys and elementary school students joined the thousands of protestors in Birmingham. Police used dogs, tear gas, and high-powered fire hoses to try to stop the peaceful demonstrators. TV cameras captured the horrible things that happened. Americans everywhere were angry.

# How did the government react to the terrible events in Birmingham?

President John F. Kennedy proposed a law to ban segregation in all public places. In support, Dr. King led the March on Washington and gave his famous "I Have a Dream" speech. Congress passed the Civil Rights Act in 1964.

# What did Dr. King receive for his work for civil rights?

In 1964, he was awarded the Nobel Peace Prize. Four years later, the Civil Rights hero was assassinated by a white racist. Today, we honor Dr. King by a national holiday on the third Monday in January, which is often near January 15, his birthday.

# Neil A. Armstrong
## 1930 – 2012

## What did President John F. Kennedy promise to do before 1970?

To land a man on the moon—about 240,000 miles away.

## What happened on July 20, 1969?

As millions watched on TV, American astronaut Neil Armstrong made history. He was the first person to walk on the moon.

## What did he say to the people back on Earth?

His first words were: "That's one small step for man, one giant leap for mankind."

ARMSTRONG'S SUIT WEIGHED 138 POUNDS.

BUT IN THE MOON'S GRAVITY IT WEIGHED ONLY 30 POUNDS.

# Did Armstrong walk on the moon alone?

No. Astronaut Buzz Aldrin Jr. was with him. Buzz was the second man to walk on the moon.

## How long were they there?

The astronauts spent twenty-one hours, thirty-six minutes, and twenty-one seconds on the moon.

## What did they do for all that time?

Explore the moon's surface. They did science experiments, collected rocks to study back on Earth, took photographs, and put up an American flag.

# Did they leave anything behind?

Besides the American flag, the astronauts left a **plaque** with these words: *Here Men from the Planet Earth First Set Foot upon The Moon July 1969 A.D. We Came in Peace for All Mankind.*

# Did the astronauts leave behind anything else?

Neil Armstrong left a mark on the moon's surface: his footprints.

# What is the next goal for manned space travel?

NASA plans to send humans to set up camp on Mars by 2035.

# Cesar Chavez
## 1927 – 1993

## Whom did Martin Luther King Jr. inspire?

A Mexican American named Cesar Chavez. In 1962, Chavez organized California migrant farm workers. These were the men, women, and children who picked fruits and vegetables by hand. Migrant families moved from field to field to look for work. With Chavez's help, the migrant workers formed a union, called the United Farm Workers of America (UFW).

## What did Chavez and the UFW do?

Chavez and the union used nonviolent protest to fight for higher wages and better working conditions for migrant workers.

CESAR HAD TO QUIT SCHOOL AT EIGHTH GRADE.

HE ATTENDED THIRTY-SEVEN DIFFERENT SCHOOLS.

## How did migrant workers live in the 1960s?

Most lived in camps built by farm owners. Their tents and shacks had no running water or indoor plumbing. They worked long hours for about a dollar an hour in fields that were sprayed with pesticides.

## Who helped Chavez start the United Farm Workers of America?

The Mexican American social activist Dolores Huerta. Together, they used labor strikes and boycotts to show Americans everywhere the horrible living conditions of migrant workers.

# When did these terrible conditions start to change?

In 1965, Chavez and the UFW began a strike against California grape growers for better wages and working conditions. Americans everywhere were asked to boycott grapes from California until the growers settled the strike.

# What did Chavez do to bring the growers to the bargaining table?

He led a three-hundred-mile walk across California. By the end of the walk, his feet were bloody and covered with blisters. Three years later, Chavez fasted for almost a month to show the suffering of farm workers and gain support for the grape boycott.

# Did the American public help the UFW cause?

Yes, people across the country stopped eating grapes from California. They also refused to buy wine from nonunion vineyards.

# Did Chavez's nonviolence tactics work?

Yes. By 1970, the major growers had signed contracts with the UFW for higher wages and better conditions. The UFW had 50,000 members by the end of the boycott.

# How did Chavez continue to fight for farm worker's rights?

At the age of 61, Chavez fasted again, in 1988. He brought attention to the dangerous effects of pesticides on farm workers and their children.

# Glossary

**abolish**—to officially end a long-standing law or system

**achievement**—something important done by a person's own efforts

**amendment**—a change or addition made to a law

**bargaining table**—meetings in which owners and workers negotiate a labor agreement or contract

**barrier**—a problem or rule that prevents people from doing something

**boycott**—refusing to buy or use something as a way of protest

**conductor**—someone in charge of passengers on a train or a tour

**diplomat**—someone who represents his or her government in a foreign country

**ecology**—the scientific study of the way that plants, animals, and people relate to one another and to their environment

**hemorrhage**—a medical condition in which a person bleeds uncontrollably inside the body

**hostage**—someone kept as a prisoner so that another person gets what he or she wants

**human rights**—basic freedoms that many societies think every person should have to be treated in a fair, equal way

**hysterical**—unable to control your behavior or emotions

**ignite**—to make something heat up; to excite

**interchangeable**—things that can be used instead of each other

**lecture**—a long talk given to a group of people

**movement**—a group of people who share the same beliefs and who work together to achieve a goal

**navigator**—an officer on a ship or plane who plans the way it should go

**nuclear bomb**—a powerful weapon that uses atomic energy to kill people and destroy large areas

**paralyzed**—unable to move a part of your body

**permanent**—existing for a long time without change

**pesticide**—a chemical used to kill insects that destroy crops

**plaque**—a piece of flat metal or stone with writing on it to remind people of an event or person

**portrait**—a painting, drawing, or photo of a person

**reformer**—someone who works to improve a social or political system

**regulation**—an official order or rule

**repeatedly**—many times, over and over again

**reservation**—land set aside for Native Americans to live on

**secede**—to officially leave or stop being part of something

**segregated**—places that are separated by sex, race, or religion

**seminary**—a college for training priests, ministers, and rabbis

**shuffle**—to walk slowly without lifting your feet

**social activist**—a person who works hard to achieve a change in society

**solo**—done alone without help of another person

**suffrage**—the right to vote in political matters, such as national elections

**survey**—to measure and make a map of an area of land

**survive**—to continue to live

**temper tantrum**—a sudden, short period of time when a child behaves very angrily and unreasonably

**temperance**—showing self-control for a specific reason, such as not drinking alcohol because of religious beliefs

**unique**—the only one of its kind

**vibrate**—shaking continuously with very small movements